SPIDERS AROUND THE WORLD

ALL ABOUT ASIAN SIX-EYED SAND SPIDERS

Nora Livingstone and Carol Kline

Mitchell Lane
PUBLISHERS
2001 SW 31st Avenue
Hallandale, FL 33009
www.mitchelllane.com

Little Mitchie

First Edition, 2024.

Author: Nora Livingstone and Carol Kline
Designer: Ed Morgan
Editor: Morgan Brody

Little Mitchie is an imprint of Mitchell Lane Publishers.

Title: All About Six-Eyed Sand Spiders
Description: Hallandale, FL : Mitchell Lane Publishers, [2024]

Series: Spiders Around the World: Asia
Library bound ISBN: 978-1-68020-881-8
eBook ISBN: 978-1-68020-888-7

Photo credits: Cover, 6–7, 8–9, 10–11, 12–13, 18–19 Wikimedia; 4–5, 16–17, 20–21 Shutterstock

CONTENTS

The Asian Six-Eyed Sand Spider lives in the **desert**.

The Asian Six-Eyed Sand Spider is small, approximately the size of a lime. Males are smaller than females, with slimmer bodies and shorter legs.

The Asian Six-Eyed Sand Spider is yellow, brown, or reddish-brown.

Many spiders have eight eyes, but the Asian Six-Eyed Sand Spider only has six eyes. These eyes give the spider excellent vision and help it to hunt **prey**.

11

The Asian Six-Eyed Sand Spider can bury itself in the sand to help stay cool in the hot desert.

They are shy and prefer to be buried. If they are **disturbed**, they will run away and quickly bury themselves in sand as soon as possible.

The Asian Six-Eyed Sand Spider is covered in small **stiff** hair. The hair holds sand to help the spider hide. Hiding helps the spider stay safe from **predators**. Hiding helps the spider hunt for food because the prey cannot see them.

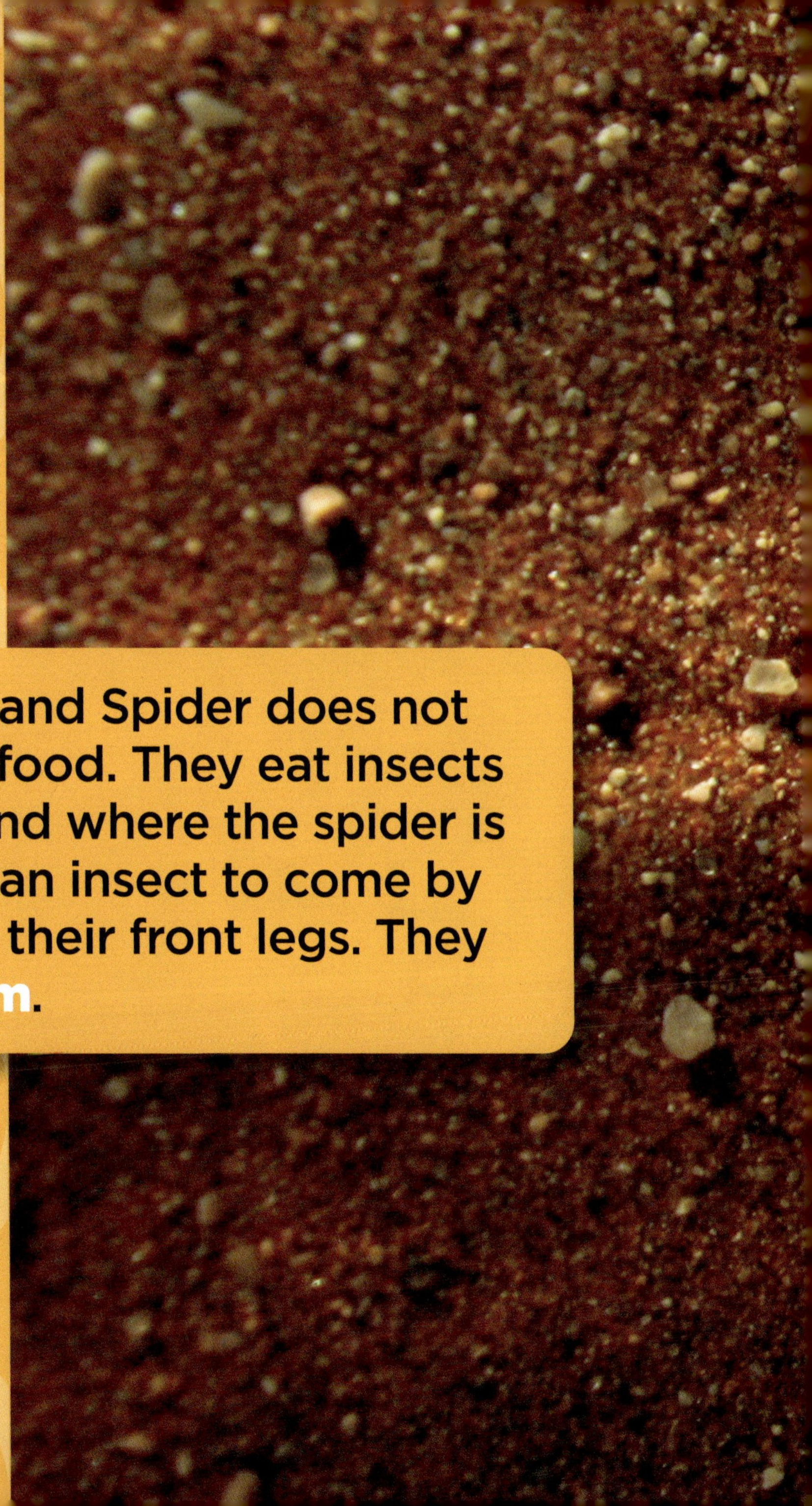

The Asian Six-Eyed Sand Spider does not build a web to catch food. They eat insects that walk over the sand where the spider is hiding. They wait for an insect to come by and they grab it with their front legs. They kill it with their **venom**.

The Asian Six-Eyed Sand Spider sleeps buried under the surface of the sand. Finding this spider can be very difficult as they are experts in **camouflage**.

Where Do **Six-Eyed Sand Spiders** Live?

Southern Asia and parts of Africa

Interesting Facts

- The Asian Six-Eyed Sand Spider's abdomen is flat and close to the ground which makes it easier to become buried in sand quickly.
- Their venom is more **toxic** than that of any other spider.
- The Asian Six-Eyed Sand Spider also eats scorpions.
- These spiders are eaten by birds and small reptiles.
- The Asian Six-Eyed Sand Spider is a carnivore as it primarily eats other animals.
- The Asian Six-Eyed Sand Spider can survive up to one year without food or water.
- This spider can live to be 15 years old.

Parts of the Spider

Abdomen
The abdomen of a spider is their belly. It contains all their guts, reproductive organs, heart, and silk glands.

Eyes
The Asian Six-Eyed Spider has six eyes.

Fangs
The Asian Six-Eyed Sand Spider has two fangs in front of its mouth.

Feelers
The Asian Six-Eyed Sand Spider has two feelers at the front of their abdomen. They are used like **antennae** to understand the world.

Head
A spider's head is where its mouth, fangs, feelers, and legs are attached.

Legs
The Asian Six-Eyed Sand Spider has eight legs.

Glossary

antennae
Sensory organs located on the head used for touch and smell

camouflage
The way animals blend or hide into their environment so they can't be seen

desert
A place that has very little rainfall. It is very hard for plants and animals to live there

disturbed
If an animal is disturbed it means their normal state has been changed and they are bothered.

prey
An animal that is hunted or killed by another animal for food

predators
An animal that hunts other animals for food

stiff
Something that is not easily bent

toxic
Poisonous

venom
A poisonous fluid that is used to defend the spider or hunt its prey. Venom from spiders is normally injected through fangs.

On the Internet

Six-eyed Sand Spider. Branson's Wild World.
http://bransonswildworld.com/six-eyed-sand-spider/

Fun Six Eyed Sand Spider Facts For Kids. Kidadl.
https://kidadl.com/facts/animals/six-eyed-sand-spider-facts

Index